l the Saga Generation

Fresh Expressions of Church for Ageing Baby Boomers

Chris Harrington

Church Army Evangelist
Associate Minister, St John the Baptist, Spalding, Lincs

GROVE BOOKS LIMITED
RIDLEY HALL RD CAMBRIDGE CB3 9HU

Contents

Acknowledgments

Many thanks to colleagues from Church Army's Older People's Focus Group (2005–7) and Mike, Steve and Claire from the Sheffield Centre who helped to develop the material in this booklet. Also to Will and Jim for their helpful red pens, and the people of the Anglican parishes of St John the Baptist and Deeping St Nicholas in Lincolnshire for the context and inspiration.

The Cover Illustration is by www.JPCreativeMedia.com

First Impression August 2008

ISSN 1367-0840

ISBN 978 1 85174 695 8

Who Are the Saga Generation? 1

You have probably heard of Saga holidays, Saga magazine and maybe even Saga radio, which are aimed at those aged fifty and over—but what about Saga Church?[1]

That is because there is not one. If there was what would it look like? When and where would it meet? Who would belong to it? Such questions have recently begun to open up an area that appears to have become a mission blind spot in the UK—the ageing baby boomer generation (1945–65).[2] They were once described as the 'first teenagers,' but are now becoming the new 'Saga generation.' Having been born in 1957 myself, I am taking about 'my generation.'

For a number of years after the Second World War there was a boom in the number of new babies being born, hence the term the 'baby boomers.' They were born into a brave new world of greater affluence, with a British welfare system that promised to provide a security net for everyone from the 'cradle to the grave.' It was a time of incredible change, so rapid that it caught the previous generations by surprise. With formative years shaped by the huge cultural changes of the late 1950s and 1960s, their attitudes and values were in sharp contrast to the generations born before the Second World War. They began to usher in the post-modern culture in which we all now swim. A social revolution had begun.

The 'baby boomers' were born into a brave new world of incredible change

Changing values and attitudes were fuelled by music that some even thought had come from the devil. The previous generation, brought up with the Christian values of Victorian Britain, could not keep up, or comprehend why or what was happening. Suddenly everything was being challenged and torn down bit by bit. Baby boomers grew up in a new world where traditional Christianity was being rejected. Elvis became king, and Dylan the prophet. The Beatles and the Rolling Stones became the heralds of a new gospel, where 'all you need is love' and the eleventh commandment was 'Let it rock.' Soon, there were converts all over the western world as television and pirate radio stations carried the message of liberation and freedom to the young and hungry masses.

At the time, a number of churches tried to give the youngsters what they wanted—coffee bars, discos, youth clubs and rock bands in the nave. But the traditional parishioners could not adjust to the changes in volume, skirts, morals and behaviour. Their barrage of complaints soon forced leaders and churches to think again. Within a few years, almost two hundred years after Sunday schools first opened, 'the salvation industry was shutting its doors to an entire generation of youngsters.'[3] The generation gap widened as values, attitudes and expectations changed.

Forty years on, many in that 'wayward' generation are now enjoying lifestyles previous generations could only dream about. Riding on the waves of consumerism and advances in technology, their boat really does seem to have come in. Huge increases on the stock exchange, generous pension payouts, property left by departed parents and a boom in the housing market have left many baby boomers very comfortably off. A recent study by pension company Friends Provident suggests that '80% of the UK's wealth belongs to the over 50s.'[4] The study also found that six out of ten retired people said they had the freedom to do what they wanted with their lives and more than half said they were able to pursue their own interests.

80% of the UK's wealth belongs to the over 50s

Many of these baby boomers are finding they really have 'never had it so good,' and they are determined to enjoy every moment of it. So it is no surprise to find companies now re-targeting these baby boomers as they get older. 'Some firms are already waking up to the fact that while youth culture might be "cool," it is far cooler to profit from the well-heeled baby boomers.'[5] Of course not everyone from the baby boomer generation falls into the specific grouping of white, middle class, well educated, 'cash rich' and 'time rich,' targeted by the Saga group of companies and others.[6] For those who do, however, it is no longer simply business as usual, as 'the financial clout they wield will be less important than the novel ways in which they want to spend their money—and what they will expect in return.'[7]

What are the Saga Generation Like?

Research into the ageing baby boomer generation in Britain by the independent think-tank Demos in 2004 highlighted three core themes.[8] These 'will help change the way that many of our everyday institutions, from banking to healthcare, are organized and delivered.'[9] First, life begins again at 50. The so-called 'mid-life crisis' is in many ways a baby boomer phenomenon. The linear social expectations of education, work, parenthood and retirement of the previous generation are being rejected in favour of 'life as a never-ending cycle, which enables them to seamlessly dip in and out of periods of education, work and leisure.'[10] Freedom and choice are the key values in the determination to enjoy life to the full for as long and as flexibly as possible. Increased wealth has provided many with a greater sense of autonomy over decisions about work and lifestyle. Some now opt for part-time working or early retirement. For the well off it is a second chance to live the dream, of motorbikes, sports cars, expensive guitars, sharp clothes, and seasons in the sun. Toys for the boys have become the new hobbies for men. Such 'toys,' as diverse as Harley Davidson motorbikes and Hornby train sets, are now being sold mainly to older consumers.

Secondly, traditional associations and stereotypes of old age are being forcefully rejected. 'The over–50s also believe they are ageing less rapidly than their parents and typically say they feel five years younger than their age.'[11] A brief look at those on the cover of any recent Saga magazine shows why. People like Brian Ferry, Ringo Starr, Jane Seymour, Harrison Ford and Honor Blackman are the new faces of the Saga generation, and looking very different from those of previous generations at the same age. Back in 1964 Bob Dylan challenged us to see that 'the times they are a changing.' Ten years later he wrote a song that could be a prophetic blessing for the Saga generation—'May you stay forever young.'[12] The '60s fashion icon, Twiggy, is once again the marketing man's dream. Beauty products are now on older women like '60s film star Jane Fonda. Holding back the years has become a growing preoccupation for both women and men in their fifties and sixties with the money to afford the new elixirs of life.

Thirdly, although ageing is a natural part of life, they are far more fearful of it than previous generations. For them, 'old age' is being pushed far into the future. Descriptive terms like 'senior,' 'older or active adult,' even 'baby boomer' are strongly rejected in favour of 'middle aged.' Old age is now thought of as 80+. A fear is growing of being sidelined, made redundant, and especially of being thought a burden to younger generations. It is interesting to note that employment legislation has only recently been introduced to combat the growing prejudice of 'ageism,' no doubt because of pressure by the Saga generation.

They are far more fearful of ageing than previous generations

They are downsizing, simplifying, and 'detoxing' their lifestyles, relocating and making financial plans for an easier future. Important issues like long term nursing care for the infirm elderly, assisted dying and palliative care are also now on the agenda of the Saga generation, whose parents are now in their 70s, 80s and 90s. Radical changes in the way death is being marked and celebrated are also starting to transform the funeral industry.

Such shifts in social trends never fail to catch the eye of politicians, who are also now trying to woo the grey voters. 'Never have the votes of people over 50 been more important to the result of the General Election. With less than a third of young people expected to turn out and vote in the forthcoming election, it's the Saga generation that will decide who wins.'[13] However, politicians are beginning to realize that the Saga generation are not going to 'put up and do their duty,' as previous generations may have done. These are the ageing eco warriors and CND campaigners who are still militant and 'crazy after all these years.' Some are crazy enough even to go to prison if they have to for their political, ethical and social beliefs. They might be entering old age, but not without a fight.

It seems ironic that the first generation to awaken mission thinking about 'generation gaps' has now been largely forgotten by the church as it has grown older. Is not it time for the church to wake up to these important social changes too?

Why No Saga Church? 2

Why have the baby boomers drifted off the mission radar of the church?

There are I believe a number of reasons. First, there may be an assumption that they have already been reached. With many traditional and rural British churches now made up of ageing congregations, some may consider that 'Saga Church' is a rather apt description, especially of the Church of England. But take another look around at the congregations of local churches in your area. You might find that although there could be a few active members in their 50s and early 60s, the majority of older members are likely to have been born before 1940—a generation who were part of Britain's last great church going revival.[14]

Secondly, churches that have engaged with outreach to older people have generally tended to focus on those born before WWII and especially to the more infirm elderly in residential care and nursing homes. Lunch clubs and services in residential care and nursing homes are vitally important and a sadly neglected ministry, which needs encouraging. However, even they only reach a small minority of older people, and certainly not the Saga generation. If anything, the baby boomers are often the ones who are engaged in and offering such ministries.

The third, and most important, reason why the Saga generation and other older generations tend to get ignored is because of the desperate cry heard in many churches—'This church needs more *younger* people.' As important as children, teenagers and young families are to the future of the church, has this cry turned into a mission mantra that we blindly chant? By taking on board the message and general attitude that evangelism is primarily about reaching the young, many older members of our churches have become de-motivated in the task of mission. This is because they have found it virtually impossible to reach across the huge generation and cultural gaps to reach young people. No wonder, then, for many church leaders trying to get their congregations enthused for mission and evangelism, it has felt like pushing a boulder up hill.

Many older members of our churches have become de-motivated in the task of mission

Jesus' promise was that his yoke is easy and his load is light (Matt 11.29–30), so why yoke older congregations to unrealistic burdens in evangelism? It is totally unrealistic to expect elderly congregations to attract young people. Why not encourage people to reach out to those of their own generation and plan outreach events and services to suit? The first step might be simply to stop chanting the mantra that we need the young.

Who are We Really Reaching?

It is time to be realistic and reflect upon the question—who are we really reaching? I recently spoke to a young Anglican ordinand who admitted that although his church had been doing a lot of outreach to children, teenagers and young families, the only people they were really reaching effectively, by default, were older people. So why not take an honest and realistic look at your congregation, or even better do a congregational audit? Make the focus of mission the people you reach naturally; it might prove far more effective.

If you already have younger families in your church, you will probably make sure there are suitable generational groups for them to be part of. Young people need role models amongst their own peers in order to encourage and inspire them in their discipleship. This might mean developing links to another church's youth group if you do not have one in your church. It seems pointless for every church to try and start a youth group when there is a perfectly good one at the church down the road. The best people to reach the young are the young themselves, those who have grown up in the church and are familiar with the different cultures the young inhabit. It is good to see specific youth congregations and cells now being planted as fresh expressions of church in their own right, like Soul Survivor in Watford. In the same way, why not develop fresh expressions of church for the Saga generation, or at least small groups and events that might help to connect with them?

The best people to reach the young are the young themselves

Some, of course, find the idea of making certain groups the focus of their outreach an anathema. After all, the kingdom of God is made up of all kinds of people, from every nation, tribe and tongue, and the message of Jesus transcends all boundaries. This is good kingdom theology. As St Paul pointed out, 'As many of you as were baptized into Christ have clothed yourself with Christ. There is no longer Jew or Greek, there is no longer slave or free, there is no longer male and female; for all are one in Christ Jesus' (Gal 3.27–28). However, the mission practice of the church has frequently had to become more narrowly focused. The book of Acts shows how the Holy Spirit led the apostles to adopt different evangelistic strategies for reaching different people with the message of the gospel. St Paul also had to admit, 'I have become all things to all people, that I might by all means save some' (1 Cor 9.22b).

Church growth research demonstrates that, in practice, churches grow more rapidly when they evangelize 'one tribe' at a time. This has become known as the Homogeneous Unit Principle (HUP), with a unit being defined as a section or sub-section of society which shares common characteristics of ethnic origins, geography, language, economic standing, class or social background. This particular church growth principle was developed in the 1970s by members of the School of World Mission at Fuller Theological Seminary, California, but its roots are in the observations of missionary anthropologists Donald McGavran and Charles Kraft in the 1960s.

Using their experience of work with different tribes on the mission field, McGavran and Kraft began to observe the radical changes in values, behaviour and attitude between the baby boomer generation and the pre-war generations. They discovered that people are less likely to become Christians if they have to cross social and cultural barriers.[15] One of the earliest and most radical responses to the 'generation gap problem' was the so-called Jesus Movement, emerging around 1967 in California. It was in many ways a foundational movement. Its influence was felt around the world, helping to inspire 'a new stream of writing, debate and action on generational divisions—a stream which has continued to flow through the Western church down to the present.'[16]

People are less likely to become Christians if they have to cross social and cultural barriers

Evangelism Across the Generations

There is not the space in this small booklet to explore the arguments of church growth principles, or those of its critics. Personally, I am persuaded by the pragmatic reasons and biblical evidence of its use in mission and evangelism, but not in its long-term orientation for churches. However, most of the books I have read on evangelism across the generations have been written with an emphasis on reaching new emerging younger generations, not older ones. Surely all social and evangelistic events, services and groups need to be tailored to fit particular contexts and contacts whatever the age, so why not older age groups like the Saga generation? For those who do want to explore these arguments further, see the 2002 report by the Evangelical Alliance—*God and the Generations: Youth, Age and the Church Today.*[17]

Having said all that, a church aimed at the Saga generation does not mean a church full of older people, or one that only caters for ageing baby boomers. An important point the Demos research highlighted was that although they need to be reached in particular ways, it would be counterproductive 'to target them overtly or to single them out as a social group.'[18] 'What struck us about the British baby boomers was their lack of interest in being part of a social club of people their own age. What they feared most of all was being marginalized or excluded.'[19] So events, activities and groups designed to reach out to the Saga generation need to be open and attractive to other generations too. It would therefore be a serious mistake to call them 'Saga Church,' or anything else that emphasizes older age.

From my own observations, it seems that a number of children in our churches appear to have been reached through grandparents bringing them to church and holiday clubs, rather than their busy parents. The age range at rock concerts these days is across the board, with baby boomer parents and their teenage children and grandchildren often enjoying the same music. This was something unheard of in the 1950s, 60s or 70s. Many of the megastars of the rock world are those of the ageing baby boomer generation, whose music is now being discovered and appreciated by younger generations. Reaching out to the Saga generation, therefore, might become a catalyst for reaching other generations.

Research from the Joseph Rowntree Foundation also found that a number of those in the Saga generation have three generations of family needing their time and resources—children, grandchildren and elderly parents. They might be juggling a number of different hats. Although two thirds were in paid employment, 'as many as one in three looked after an elderly relative or friend, one in six provided care for a grandchild and one in ten did both.'[20] Churches that are trying to attract the Saga generation therefore need to take note that regular attendance on a weekly basis is also unlikely.

The Church Needs More Older People

3

The kingdom of God has been described as the 'upside down kingdom,' so why not turn the cry of 'this church needs more younger people' on its head?[21]

'This church needs more older people.' Now that really would be a radical mission statement for a church!

In fact it was this headline on the Church Army magazine *In Touch* back in 1999 that made me re-assess my own thinking about mission. The article that went with it, by Church Army captain Alan Barr, helped me to re-focus and include older people in my future mission strategies.[22] With a background in engineering and the music industry, I came to faith at the age of 30 and was commissioned as a Church Army evangelist in 2002, when I entered full-time ministry as the associate minister and community evangelist at two Anglican churches in the Lincolnshire Fens. Located in one of the parishes were five residential care/nursing homes, two communities of elderly people in sheltered accommodation and a day centre run by Age Concern. The churches both had older congregations and so I intentionally made older people an important part of the focus of my outreach ministry. During that time I also began to reflect on how younger generations might cope with the ageing process.

I began to imagine what residential care/nursing homes would be like in ten to fifteen years' time once my own generation began to need such care. We definitely will not be asking for music by Daniel O'Donnell, Jim Reeves and Vera Lynn, or want the local church to come in singing traditional old hymns. It will be, 'Nurse can you put on Pink Floyd, the Beatles, the Stones, or Led Zeppelin, and can we see the latest DVD?' (or whatever the new technology is by then). I also do not believe baby boomers will be as passive in their old age as other generations have been. Things will change, and perhaps quite radically. Even now perceptions are changing and older voices are being heard, sometimes in an unusual way.

Perceptions are changing and older voices are being heard

In early 2007 a television documentary was made about some unlikely pop stars, 'The Zimmers,' an aptly named group of British pensioners in their

80s, 90s and older who recorded a new version of The Who's old hit 'My Generation.' As a protest song at the way older people are being treated, Pete Townsend's words come across as just as stinging. After receiving over two million hits on the Internet site *YouTube,* radio stations were forced into playing it, and The Zimmers climbed the charts.

Thinking for a moment about the pre-Saga generation, visiting residential care and nursing homes is a valuable, rewarding and relatively easy ministry for ordinary church members. Yet even that tends to get missed off the mission agenda of many churches. Perhaps it is seen by some as a waste of time and effort, forgetting that some of the people now in residential care homes and nursing homes were once prominent members of our churches. According to Mike Collyer of the Sheffield Centre, Church Army's research unit, 'Anecdotal evidence suggests that it only takes five weeks for an older person to become de-churched following a time of absence through illness or hospitalization. Institutional ageism within the church needs to be challenged.'[23] Nor is it much of a witness, either to the families of those in residential care, or to the staff.

Some of the people now in residential care homes were once prominent members of our churches

However, with only around 4% of older people in residential care, it would be a mistake to assume the church is doing well with its mission to older people because of its ministry in care homes.[24] What about the other 96% of older people? Where are they to be found? Living at home, or with their children, out working, or perhaps on a Saga holiday somewhere. 'One of the myths rife in this country is that all old people are the same.'[25] Older people are as diverse a group as younger people; they also span a very wide age range and many are not being reached at all.

For over a hundred years, Church Army has been one of the few mission organizations putting faith into action in its practical outreach to older people. Having now closed the last of its residential care homes, its ministry to older people is primarily focused through the work of Church Army evangelists in Anglican parish settings. This is often worked out in practice through a ministry to residential care and nursing homes and in helping set up and run parish-based lunch clubs. However, like other mission agencies, it too needs to reach a new and very different generation.

Fresh Expressions for Older People

The Church of England's report, *Mission-Shaped Church,* published in 2004, has encouraged the development of fresh expressions of church for the vast majority of the population who are either un-churched or de-churched.[26] The following year, Church Army's Older People's Focus Group, of which I was a member, decided to broaden its vision and think about fresh expressions of church for older people. The title for the focus group conference was 'Saga Church.' I had floated this idea after thinking about the 'other 96%' of older people not in residential care or nursing homes and the new generation reading the Saga magazine. Steve Hollinghurst of the Sheffield Centre produced a thought provoking PowerPoint presentation on the values and attitudes of the Saga Generation, to help us look, and listen again, to the music, historical events and social changes that transformed Britain in a generation.[27] The differences in values and outlook across an age range of forty years, from those in their 50s to those in their 90s, immediately became clear.

The conference became a catalyst for a fresh look at this relatively unexplored area of mission, with a second conference picking up the same theme the following year. Mike Collyer, who was the focus group convenor for many years, and is now part of the research team at the Sheffield Centre, collated much of the material from these two conferences into a report, called '*What Church for the Saga Generation? Cultural Shifts in the Younger Old.*'[28] It was published as part of Mike's *Discovering Faith in Later Life* series.[29] Several one-day conferences also followed at the Wilson Carlile College of Evangelism in Sheffield as part of the VOX forum.[30]

One of the few other home mission agencies that is committed to offering Christian hope and encouragement for older people and who have resources specifically targeted to reaching older people, including the Saga generation, is the Outlook Trust.[31] Launched in 1992 by Rhena Taylor, a missionary in Africa from 1962–90, with a vision to reach out to older people, headlines in the Christian press said, 'A new mission to reach the over 50s for Christ.' Visionary stuff indeed, back in 1992.

The ageing generation needs its own fresh expressions of church

In America and Australia the changing needs of the baby boomer generation have been on the church agenda for some time. In Britain, the idea that this ageing generation might need its own fresh expressions of church is still in its infancy. The Baptist Union is one of the few church denominations to have developed mission resources.[32]

4 A Generation of Spiritual Seekers

> We are stardust, we are golden,
> and we've got to get ourselves back to the garden.[33]

According to sociologist Callum Brown, the massive cultural changes that took place in Britain from the 1960s onwards drastically altered the social mechanism of passing on the values and beliefs of Christianity from one generation to the other. As a result, the baby boomer generation failed to absorb Christianity into their lives as part and parcel of their identity as British people.[34] Although regular opinion polls appear to show that British people still believe in God, what they believe about God is far from clear. British people are becoming disconnected from their Christian roots as churches decline not only in size, but also in moral standing. Generations since the 1960s have simply lost contact in the church. Brown's analysis and prediction of the death of Christian Britain is challenging and sobering reading. We might not agree with Brown's prognosis of imminent death, but we have to admit that all is not well with the patient.

The Christianity of the pre-war generation might have been steadily rejected, but it has left a spiritual hole in people's lives. A new spiritual quest now appears to be on. But that search for spiritual meaning seems to be passing the Christian churches by. Perhaps because of their mistrust of institutions, the Saga generation, like all the other post war generations, seems to be going everywhere except to church in their spiritual quest for meaning. A number of writers in America and Australia have begun to stimulate the debate on this issue including Wade Clark Roof[35] and David Tacey.[36] Tacey's challenging work is now being analysed in the British context. Paul Heelas and Linda Woodhead explored *The Spiritual Revolution,* based on research in Kendal in the Lake District,[37] and Yvonne Richmond has also done extensive research into the spirituality of people outside the church in the Diocese of Coventry.[38]

With a post-modern aversion to absolutes, many from the Saga generation have developed a pick and mix approach to spirituality. Michael Reiter argues that, although encouraging, this wind of change is not one that we should blindly accept as a work of the Holy Spirit, and offers a helpful, critical analysis, from an evangelical perspective. In *Stirrings of the Soul,* Reiter highlights some of the key elements in many of the spiritualities on offer, which are being tried in the growing search for meaning.[39]

- Hunger for relationships and a sense of connectedness with God, the cosmos and others.
- A thirst for experience—searching for an encounter with the divine that will touch their souls.
- Non-rational—unable to explain rationally, but looking for that 'Aha' feeling.
- Non-judgmental and non-restrictive, wanting to be helped and affirmed not criticized or judged
- Inclusive and pluralistic—rejecting exclusivist truth claims—'it's OK if it works for you.'
- Everyday spirituality, affecting every part of life with ethical demands to liberate others.
- Marketplace spirituality offering greater choice to find a spirituality that suits them.
- Therapeutic benefits, bringing healing and wholeness to the physical, emotional and psychological scars of life.
- Inner-directed spirituality focused on the human spirit within us, not the God outside us.

Reiter suggests that, 'devotees of the new spirituality are largely members of the post-war generation and their offspring.' How can churches address this hunger and interest in spirituality? How can disaffected baby boomers respond to their growing spiritual experiences and find their way 'back to the garden'? Part of that answer could be by developing fresh expressions of church, so that the Saga generation can hear the life-changing gospel of Jesus without some of the negative baggage they might associate with traditional churches.

5 Fresh Expressions, Stories and Ideas

In March 2007, a special envisioning day was held at Lincoln Cathedral for people from across Lincolnshire to discover more about fresh expressions of church.

It was an ecumenical event led the national Fresh Expressions team and highlighting what local churches in the area were already doing. What was interesting was that well over half the people who attended were from the Saga generation, who were either doing, or were interested in starting, some kind of fresh expression of church. On the stall I had taken, highlighting initiatives in Spalding, I also had a small display with some recent covers of *Saga Magazine* and the question—'Saga Holidays, Saga Magazine, Saga Church?' It generated quite a bit of interest, with many wanting to know more, as well as admitting that they too were now part of the Saga generation. I had to confess that, as yet, there was not a 'Saga Church' in Britain, but posed the question—why not? And what would it look like?

Some might imagine a cross between the enthusiastic congregations featured in the films *Sister Act* and *Blues Brothers*, with the Revd Al Green as the pastor, U2 as the in-house praise band and Bob Geldof heading up the events committee, meeting in a solar powered, eco-friendly, church building, complete with a gym and health spa! Sadly, in the real world, such images are likely to remain the fantasy of filmmakers. What is true is that one size no longer fits all, and different things will work for different kinds of baby boomers in different contexts.

As far as I am aware, at the time of writing there is not a church in Britain that has been started to specifically aim at reaching the Saga generation. Some may have found that they are, but by default rather than by design. In the United States it is a different story. There, baby boomers have been much more vocal in articulating their needs and interests, which has led to sustained research into their values over a number of years. One of the problems in thinking about British baby boomers is that 'very little research has addressed them directly.'[40] There may be generalized lessons to be learnt from American research, but it must

There is not a church in Britain thatspecifically aims at reaching the Saga generation

be remembered that Britain is a different context and culture with a very different history of church going. However, there are a number of good books on this subject from an American perspective, one of which lists ten general criteria for attracting (American) baby boomers.[41, 42] Given the findings of the Demos research, this may also prove to be a useful list of points that are worth being aware of.

1 De-emphasize membership—boomers are not joiners; they attend church to experience something, and to participate, but do not like joining institutions.

2 Do not expect blind institutional loyalty—a church that is conveniently located and accommodates their needs takes precedence over denominational loyalty.

3 Accommodate their desire for experience—having grown up in an experience orientated age, they seek a real sense of God's presence in their lives.

4 Emphasize 'how to' messages—they want to know how God can make a difference in their lives. Relevant topics could be how to have a happier marriage, handle money better, deal with stress at work, be a better parent—and so on.

5 Recognize the importance of equality in roles of leadership, authority and responsibility—boomers have campaigned for equality in society and expect it in the church.

6 Accept and celebrate the contribution of singles—especially with divorce rates rising and some now having lost their partner through death.

7 Respond to the relatively high level of dysfunctionality and emotional pain—many boomers have been through some very stressful times that have left them with emotional scars and wounds.

8 Innovation and activities—they embrace change and applaud innovation, like diversity and options. They have a sense of destiny and want to make a difference in the world.

9 Encourage discussion, not dogma—baby boomers are known as the 'hinge generation' with respect to the transition from modernism to post modernism and have a blend of modern and post-modern values and belief systems that favour pluralism rather than absolutes.

10 It is imperative to communicate in the right musical language—music is the language we grow up with. It is the soundtrack to our lives. It changes from generation to generation and defines who we are. John Wimber, a 1960s rock musician, helped to develop the identity of the Vineyard Church around music; so too has Rick Warren at Saddleback Church.

In the early 1990s, John Finney did some research into how people came to faith in this country.[43] Although Finney's research was not age specific in its remit, many of the stories recounted are by people who, fifteen years on since its publication, are now part of the Saga generation. There are a number of lessons to be learnt from reading these stories again with regards to making connections and helping to build faith. Especially important is Finney's observation that new images/icons of God/Christ need to be used in communicating the gospel to baby boomers wary of the emphasis on the 'turn or burn' message they heard when they were teenagers.

Baby boomers are wary of the emphasis on the 'turn or burn' message

The Saga generation is one that does not trust governments, multinationals, institutions or authority figures to give them advice, and is cynical about branding. They dislike being patronized, dictated to or condescended to, demanding honesty, consistency, reliability, quality, value for money and good service. The recent television series, *Grumpy Old Men and Women*, which consists of ageing baby boomers moaning about what gets them angry in society, confirms the Demos research.

What follows is a number of ideas that might help churches put some of these findings into action and help the church to connect with the Saga generation. Throughout this book I have written in general terms about the baby boomer generation. We are not all the same. Only through research and experimentation in your own particular context will you really discover whether they help the individual baby boomers you have contact with to experience Christ for themselves.

Willow Creek Seeker Services

One church that has been successful in reaching baby boomers in the US is the Willow Creek Community Church, based in a suburb of Chicago.[44] Although it is now one of the biggest churches in the US, it started in 1975 when its founder, Bill Hybels, and the team with him, specifically aimed at reaching those in the same baby boom generation as themselves. After specific market research highlighted the kind of church they might come to, Willow Creek began, not in a traditional church building, but in a suburban movie theatre, free from traditional religious symbols. With a rock band providing the music, and the slick use of drama, followed by a talk by Hybels on a specific life issue, the hour-long service is more like a presentation (which lasts one hour), than a worship service. It is tailored specifically to un-churched or de-churched seekers, rather than traditional churchgoers. These 'seeker services' are held at the weekend. In the week its members are encouraged to join small groups for Bible teaching and discipleship training.

Encouraged by Willow Creek's success, some churches have tried the 'seeker service' format in this country. They have not been primarily aimed at the Saga generation, but younger age groups. It needs a capable group of musicians, a polished drama group and an inspirational speaker. Unfortunately, such resources are hard to come by, and are absent in many local churches in Britain, which is one of the reasons why I think seeker services have not caught on to any great extent in this country. Nevertheless, the general idea could be well worth trying by those serious about reaching the Saga generation and have the resources needed. However, what most churches forget is the amount of research that went on at Willow Creek in order to tailor their services to those they wanted to reach, before they opened their doors.

The Big Picture

One of the churches in the UK that does have the musical resources and inspirational speakers to do Willow Creek style seeker services is St Andrew's, Chorleywood. With speakers such as J John and Mark Stibbe, they have used a seeker service type format using film clips to attract people and illustrate the Christian message. According to the books written about these particular series of services, *The Big Picture,* the format they used for a series of ninety-minute services using films, was as follows:

Welcome and introduction
Prayer
Trailer for movie
Songs
Talk—illustrated with clips from the movie
Dance/drama/song
Testimony or reading
Song
Appeal
Prayer ministry
Blessing
Refreshments

Hundreds of people were attracted to this type of service using popular films to provide contemporary illustrations to 'issue specific' messages. 'Often movies move us in a way that no other form of communication can—in fact some people consider movies to be the parables of life today. Movies are a great way of getting us to think about life's ultimate questions.'[45] These ideas, including the actual talks and clips themselves, can be found in the books, *The Big Picture* and *The Big Picture 2.* Though this series of film-illustrated talks is not specifically aimed at those from the Saga generation, it would certainly appeal to their love of the movies.

Reel Issues—A Film and Faith Group

Taking the title from a book by Ian Mayer, on using film to explore contemporary issues, like many others, I have run a film and faith group in our local church.[46] It ran for about three years, meeting twice a month in someone's home during the autumn and winter, the first week to watch the entire film together and the following week to watch some clips and discuss the issues raised. Although it was a small group of eight to ten, the vast majority were from the Saga generation. The group began with a Lent course based on the film *Chocolat,* called *Christ and the Chocolaterie* by Hilary Brand.[47] It was an excellent course and gave us a good format for a regular film and faith group in which each member of the group chooses a film and leads the discussion. This could be used specifically to reach out to those from the Saga generation and there is plenty of good film material around which touches issues affecting and interesting them. (See the extra resources section for this book on the Grove Books website for a list of relevant films and other resources to help you reach out to the Saga generation.)[48]

'The Well' and Other Small 'Transforming Communities'

Steven Croft's book, *Transforming Communities,* has a helpful critique on several popular methods of evangelism and new models of church.[49] Croft offers his own model, using small groups to transform the community they are part of, like the yeast that eventually leavens the whole lump in Jesus' parable.[50] I decided to form such a group to see if God would bring about such a transformation in the two churches I was part of.

With a hunger to belong, to develop, and to explore the spiritual aspects of life high on the agenda of baby boomers, it was perhaps no surprise to find that it was mainly people in their early fifties who responded to an advertisement I placed in the parish magazine. It read, '*The Well*: A place to be refreshed, to find refreshment for others, to encounter Christ and to draw out living water, a place of discovery, a place on the way, a deep place, a sacred place, a place of peace.'

One of the turning points came *via* the *Essence* course by Rob Frost, which had a deep and powerful effect upon the whole group.[51] Experiential and tactile, this course was designed for all who recognize they are on a spiritual journey and who want to explore that journey with others. Drawing on the teachings of Jesus, the Christian mystics and environmental concerns, this is a course baby boomers can really connect with. It is not designed to tell the whole Christian story, but picks up on issues such as community and belonging, image and identity, ecology and stewardship, emotional pain and wholeness, seeking God, prayer and meditation. It has lots of material, practical exercises and help setting up a group at a suitable neutral venue, as well as a CD of music and meditations.

A number of those Christian baby boomers have since gone on to train as lay parish ministers, taking the desire to bring about change for the better with them, and are still helping to bring about transformation. It worked.

Rambling Groups, Retreats and Pilgrimages

Rambling is a good way to keep fit, enjoy the countryside and meet new people, and the Ramblers Association also campaigns for greater access to the countryside for all. These are all good reasons why it appeals to those from the Saga generation. So why not organize regular church rambles that include visiting old country churches, giving an opportunity to enjoy the peace and presence of God of those places? Longer rambles could also be organized with a group staying overnight at one of the many Christian retreat centres around the country, helping to form relationships and enjoy Christian hospitality at its best. There are a number of well-known Christian pilgrimage sites around the country that also charge the imagination of non-Christians who visit, and leave a lasting impression on those searching for spiritual experiences. Friendship is the key to all these groups, with people responding to a personal invitation from a Christian friend, rather than an advert or poster. See www.ramblers.org.uk and www.retreats.org.uk for some useful information in planning.

Book Groups

Reading has become popular once again, encouraged by the burgeoning book group scene popularized by TV chat show hosts, Richard and Judy. We are all attracted by stories and, like film and faith groups, novels are a way of getting people chatting about the big issues that affect us all. Having started a book group at the local church, I was surprised to find that those who responded to an article in the parish magazine were all baby boomers. Why not invite friends or work colleagues to read a book together and meet at a local coffee shop to discuss it? There are some great books around, and whatever the venue, they can provide the neutral ground on which to meet to discuss faith issues and life experiences.

Body, Mind and Soul—Holistic Fitness

With health and well being near the top of the agenda for many ageing baby boomers, a good way to reach out to them is to start a keep fit group with a difference. One local church in Spalding began a group that met weekly to discuss topical issues in the news and have a time of prayer as well as to do some physical exercise like a game of badminton. Why not start a keep fit or line-dancing group at your church and provide an opportunity for spiritual input too, perhaps in the form of silent meditation and contemplation from a Christian perspective, as well as social times?

Community Ministry—Active Religion with Purpose

Making a difference in the world is what many of the Saga generation still aspire to. Religion that has purpose beyond Bible study, prayer and praise services is what some still expect Christianity to be about. Discipleship, with practical opportunities to make a difference, is essential if those from the Saga generation are to be reached. Several writers explore how Christians can build links with people of peace in the community by working together on projects of common ground and interest to the community.[52] Through such community projects, friendships can be made and faith shared. It is an experience that changes all parties through genuine dialogue and God's grace. Community ministry can provide an excellent way in for Christians to make and build connections with fellow baby boomers from the Saga generation who still want to make a difference and change the world via community projects.

U2charist

A recent event in Lincoln of a Communion service, that was developed in America, using the music and lyrics of the rock band U2, has led to the formation of a 'U2charist Community.' They have started a weekly lunchtime prayer café, with an act of worship at a town centre church. They too are using the community ministry approach. With the music of U2, and the eight Millennium Development Goals as a common agenda, they are hoping people of faith and no faith will rally around to see what a difference they can make locally. The concert/Communion service attracted people of all ages and really caught their imagination. Other communities are planned. See www.u2charistlincoln.org.uk for more information and links to the American site.

Acoustic Café

A church in Sidmouth in Devon started up a music evening with a difference that met in a local café/bar, offering local young songwriters and musicians a chance to play some of their own songs or cover versions on acoustic guitars, inspired by the 'unplugged' MTV idea. It attracted young and old and was something that appealed to those like me from the Saga generation. I had come across it whilst on holiday and so tried the idea for a while in my local church in Spalding. However, I found it did not transfer so well, but that may have been due to the venue (our church lounge) rather than the idea itself. At the time I pitched it at young people rather than a mixture of both young and older. In the right venue, this idea could appeal to older musicians, like me, who still enjoy playing songs from the James Taylor songbook!

Soul Food Fund Raising Socials

Social evenings helping to raise funds for good causes, featuring music appealing to boomers and home cooked curries, is another way make connections and build friendships. It can also be a chance for some to give a talk on their travels around the world, as a number have been on some amazing adventures. We have had some great evenings during Christian Aid weeks, hearing about local boomers' travels to Nepal, Vietnam and Antarctica, with food to match.

Virtual Congregations and Sacred 'Web' Space

Although baby boomers grew up using slide rule, rather than calculators or computers, they have caught on fast to the benefits of technology. Now laptops, mobile phones and even BlackBerries and Palm diaries help them stay in touch with family and friends and sift through the wealth of choice that can overwhelm consumers today. They are also more likely to engage in their spiritual search via the web than by just turning up at a church. So in designing websites, churches need to be aware of the different generations who might be logging on. There are now a growing number of virtual congregations that baby boomers are connecting with, including sites like St Pixels at www.ship-of-fools.com. Also a number of websites offer the opportunity for prayer on line, such as www.sacredspace.ie run by the Jesuits. For more information see *Online Church* in the Grove Pastoral series.

Some Other Ideas

- Encouraging creativity—art and craft, music, literature, theatre and film.
- Christian bikers' groups—living the dream and sharing faith experiences.
- Discussing faith and exploring belief critically in small groups.
- All-age worship for grandparents and grandchildren.

These are but a few of the ideas for connecting with the Saga generation that are already being explored. It is not exhaustive by any means (there are more resources connected with this book on the Grove Books website too).[53] Creative thinking in your own context will no doubt throw up many other ideas. It is, of course, vitally important to develop any ideas with, rather than for, members of the Saga generation. Any advertising should be direct and straightforward and 'do what it says on the tin.' Personal invitation is always the best way, so your baby boomers need to be happy and comfortable with the events, groups and activities eventually decided upon. Keep them involved through the whole planning and development process.

The respected Bible scholar and thinker, Walter Brueggemann, has argued that in a post-modern era where grand visions, overarching systems and meta narratives are being rejected, the Bible remains a rich resource of stories to 'fund the post-modern imagination,' providing 'the pieces, materials, and resources out of which a new world can be imagined...out of which people can put life together in fresh configurations.'[54] Demos also point out, 'In order to challenge the prevailing gloom about ageing we need to urgently invent a collective story about the value of growing older. Organizations that can assist in framing that story are likely to find a powerful and positive response.'[55]

The purpose of this book, therefore, is to challenge mission mantras and stimulate reflection, discussion and exploration. It does not have all the answers, or any wild claims of 'success.' But it does have some observations, stories and ideas that are still being worked out and put into practice, that are offered up as fragments to help stir the imagination in a post-modern era ushered in by the Saga generation.

Notes

1 These are all trade names of the Saga Group, a leisure company that specifically targets people over the age of 50.

2 Fifty is now considered the beginning of the older age groups by a number of organizations and companies.

3 C G Brown, *The Death of Christian Britain: Understanding Secularization 1800–2000* (London: Routledge, 2001) p180.

4 Headline in the *Daily Mail* on 6 April 2007 (article by Steve Doughty).

5 J Harkin and J Huber, *Eternal Youths: How the Baby Boomers are Having their Time Again* (London: Demos, 2004), p 12.

6 For more information on the Saga Group of companies visit www.saga.co.uk

7 Harkin and Huber, *op cit*, p12.

8 www.demos.co.uk

9 Harkin and Huber, *op cit*, p 13.

10 Harkin and Huber, *op cit*, p 105.

11 Reported by Steve Doughty in the *Daily Mail* on 6 April 2007.

12 From the song *Forever Young* by Bob Dylan from the album *Planet Waves* (Columbia Records, 1974).

13 Saga Group press release, 22 March 2005.

14 Brown, *op cit*, pp 170–175.

15 For more in depth information see D Hilborn and M Bird (eds), *God and the Generations: Youth, Age and the Church Today* (Carlisle: Paternoster Press, 2002), a report by the Evangelical Alliance (UK) Commission on Unity and Truth among Evangelicals (ACUTE).

16 Hilborn and Bird, *op cit*, p 5.

17 Hilborn and Bird, *op cit*.

18 Harker and Huber, *op cit*, p 95.

19 Harker and Huber, *op cit*, p 95.

20 Quoted in Harkin and Huber, *op cit*, p 79.

21 D B Kraybill, *The Upside Down Kingdom,* (Scottdale: Herald Press, 1978).

22 Capt Alan Barr CA, quoted in issue six of *Share It,* Church Army, 1999.

23 M Collyer, *What Church for the Saga Generation?,* p11.

24 Around 4% according to M Collyer in *What Church for the Saga Generation?,* p 16.

25 D Norton, in S Greengross, *Ageing: An Adventure in Living,* (Souvenir, 1985) p 45.

26 *Mission Shaped Church: Church Planting and Fresh Expressions of Church in a Changing Context* is a report from the Church of England's Mission and Public Affairs Council (London: Church House Publishing, 2004).

27 Available from Steve Hollinghurst at the Sheffield Centre.

28 For a copy of the report, contact Mike Collyer at ask@sheffieldcentre.org.uk

29 For a list of these excellent reports, which both critique and tell the story of a number of faith based projects working with older people, contact Mike Collyer at ask@sheffieldcentre.org.uk

30 VOX (Valuing Older eXperience) is a new forum with representatives from OUTLOOK trust, EA, Faith Works, Church Army, Mission Care, REGENERATE-RISE, Keychange Charity, Christian Council on Ageing and Rob Merchant, author of *Pioneering the Third Age,* and other individuals concerned with the churches' response to supporting and working with older people in faith development and mission.

31 www.outlook-trust.org.uk. See also Mike Collyer's report in his *Discovering Faith in Later Life Series, No 4*—The Outlook Trust available from ask@sheffieldcentre.org.uk

32 http://www.baptist.org.uk/resources/seniors.html

33 Lyrics from the song *Woodstock* by Joni Mitchell.

34 C G Brown, *The Death of Christian Britain: Understanding Secularism 1800–2000* (London: Routledge, 2001).

35 W C Roof, *Spiritual Marketplace: Baby Boomers and the Remaking of American Religion* (Princetown: Princetown University Press, 1999).

36 D Tacey, *The Spirituality Revolution: The Emergence of Contemporary Spirituality* (London: Brunner-Routledge, 2004).

37 P Heelas, L Woodhead, B Seel, K Tusting and B Szerszynski, *The Spiritual Revolution, Why Religion is Giving Way to Spirituality* (Oxford: Wiley-Blackwell, 2004).

38 N Spencer, *Beyond the Fringe: Researching a Spiritual Age.* This is the report of

the Rev'd Yvonne Richmond's exploration in the Diocese of Coventry into the spirituality of people outside the church (Calver: Cliff College Publishing, 2005).

39 M Reiter, *Stirrings of the Soul: Evangelicals and the New Spirituality* (Matthias Media, 2003) ch 4.

40 Harkin and Huber, *op cit*, p 12.

41 W Benke and L Benke, *The Generation Driven Church: Evangelizing Boomers, Busters and Millennials* (Cleveland: The Pilgrim Press, 2002); D Murren, *The Baby Boomerang* (Ventura: Regal Books, 1990); W C Roof, *A Generation of Seekers: The Spiritual Journeys of the Baby Boom Generation* (New York: Harper Collins, 1993); R Warren, *The Purpose Driven Church: Growth without Compromising your Message and Mission* (Grand Rapids: Zondervan, 1995).

42 Taken from D Murren, *The Baby Boomerang* (Ventura: Regal Books, 1990) and quoted in W Benke and L Benke, *The Generation Driven Church: Evangelizing Boomers, Busters and Millennials.*

43 J Finney, *Finding Faith Today: How Does it Happen?* (Swindon: British and Foreign Bible Society, 1992).

44 For more information see B Hybels and L Hybels, *Rediscovering Church: The Story and Vision of Willow Creek Community Church* (Grand Rapids: Zondervan, 1995) and G A Pritchard, *Willow Creek Seeker Services: A New Way of Doing Church* (Chicago: Baker Books, 1995).

45 J John and M Stibbe, *The Big Picture 2: Looking at the Spiritual Message from Movies,* (Milton Keynes: Authentic Lifestyle, 2003) back cover.

46 I Maher, *Reel Issues: Engaging Film and Faith* (Swindon: Bible Society, 2002). See also I Maher, *Faith and Film: Close Encounters of an Evangelistic Kind* (Grove Evangelism booklet Ev 59).

47 H Brand, *Christ and the Chocolaterie: A Lent Course* (London: Darton Longman and Todd, 2002).

48 www.grovebooks.co.uk. See also www.connectbiblestudies.com and www.hollywoodjesus.com

49 S Croft, *Transforming Communities: Re-imagining the Church for the 21st Century* (London: Darton Longman and Todd, 2002).

50 Luke 13.20–21.

51 R Frost, *Essence: An Exploration of Contemporary Spirituality Which Looks Towards a Lifestyle Integrating Body, Mind and Spirit* (Eastbourne: Kingsway Publications, 2002).

52 R Fung, *The Isaiah Vision* (Geneva: WCC Publications, 1992); A Morisy, *Beyond*

the Good Samaritan: Community Ministry and Mission (London: Mowbray, 1997); J Wallis, *The Soul of Politics: A Practical and Prophetic Vision for Change* (London: Fount/Harper Collins, 1994) and R Sider, *Bread of Life: Stories of Radical Mission* (London: Triangle/SPCK, 1994) are all books that I have found especially inspiring on community ministry.

53 www.grovebooks.co.uk; go to this book title on the website and click on extra resources.

54 W Brueggemann, *The Bible and Postmodern Imagination* (London: SCM, 1993) p 20.

55 Harkin and Huber, *op cit*, p106.